12 TIPS FOR
STAYING SAFE

by Jamie Kallio

STORY
LIBRARY

www.12StoryLibrary.com

12-Story Library is an imprint of Peterson Publishing Company and Press Room Editions.

Produced for 12-Story Library by Red Line Editorial

Photographs ©: gbh007/iStockphoto, cover, 1; 1000 Words/Shutterstock Images, 4; Dragon Images/Shutterstock Images, 5; SpeedKingz/Shutterstock Images, 6, 9; Juanmonino/ iStockphoto, 7; Halfpoint/iStockphoto/Thinkstock, 8; Amy Myers/Shutterstock Images, 10; Blend Images/Shutterstock Images, 11, 28; dotshock/Shutterstock Images, 12, 29; Rock and Wasp/Shutterstock Images, 13; Andrey Popov/Shutterstock Images, 14; Pixsooz/ iStockphoto, 16; Lisa F. Young/Shutterstock Images, 17; Syda Productions/Shutterstock Images, 18; Crutyvus Vadym/Shutterstock Images, 19; oliveromg/Shutterstock Images, 20; Steve Cukrov/Shutterstock Images, 22; Georgios Kollidas/Shutterstock Images, 23; Jaromir Chalabala/Shutterstock Images, 24; Africa Studio/Shutterstock Images, 25; Oktay Ortakcioglu/iStockphoto, 26; John Kirk/iStockphoto, 27

Library of Congress Cataloging-in-Publication Data
Cataloging-in-publication information is on file with the Library of Congress.
978-1-63235-367-2 (hardcover)
978-1-63235-385-6 (paperback)
978-1-62143-509-9 (hosted ebook)

Printed in the United States of America
Mankato, MN
May, 2016

Access free, up-to-date content on this topic plus a full digital version of this book. Scan the QR code on page 31 or use your school's login at 12StoryLibrary.com.

Table of Contents

Use Cyber Sense When on the Internet

People around the world depend on the Internet. People use it to communicate with family and friends, shop, play games, and find information. The Internet makes it easy to share interests with others. However, accessing the Internet requires caution. Not much is private on the Internet.

To protect your privacy when accessing the Internet, use cyber sense. Think of strong passwords for your e-mail and social networking accounts. A strong password should be something only you know. It should consist of different characters, numbers, and letters. Once you create a password, only share it with your parents. Another way to maintain privacy is to never post your home address or phone number on the Internet. Before sharing photos and videos, think carefully. Once something is on the Internet, it might be there

Social networking sites such as Facebook and Twitter allow friends and strangers to interact.

forever. Also, location data is often embedded in modern smartphones. This means that someone can find out where your photo was taken once you post it online.

Do not click on strange links. This will help to avoid downloading viruses. And be wary of online strangers. Never meet up with someone you've met only online. If you come across something on the Internet that makes you feel uneasy, tell a trusted adult.

3 billion

Estimated number of people who use the Internet worldwide.

- The Internet lets us connect with friends, family, and information all around the world.
- With the rise of the Internet comes a certain lack of privacy.
- Personal information and computer passwords should never be shared with other people.

Think before you post photos of you and your friends online.

Put a Stop to Bullying

Bullying deeply affects the person who is targeted. Bullying can be verbal, social, or physical. Teasing and name-calling are examples of verbal bullying. If someone tells other kids to leave you out of an activity, that is called social bullying. Physical bullying involves physically hurting someone.

Bullying can happen during school and after school hours. It can even happen online. Everyone deserves to feel safe, whether it's at school or at home behind a computer screen. To stop being bullied, or to help someone else who is being bullied, talk to a trusted adult. This can be a parent, a teacher, or a school counselor. Many schools have bullying policies. Working with the right people can help put a stop to bullying.

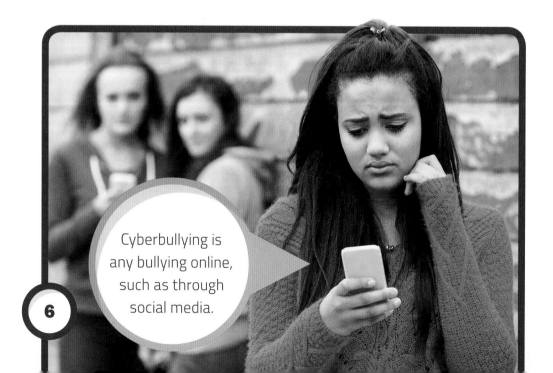

Cyberbullying is any bullying online, such as through social media.

Make an effort to comfort and support someone you see being bullied.

Sometimes people bully others because negative things are happening in their lives. They feel sad about a situation at home or worried about an issue at school. If you feel tempted to bully others, stop and think. Is something negative going on in your life that you can't control? Everyone deserves kindness and respect. If you are still feeling mean or angry and want to bully someone, talk to an adult you trust. Together you can come up with ways to deal with your feelings.

2.7 million

Estimated number of kids in the United States who experience bullying.

- Bullying can be verbal, social, physical, or cyber.
- If you witness bullying, tell a trusted adult.
- Many schools have bullying policies in place.

Be Alert and Aware of Strangers

Almost everyone has heard the phrase *stranger danger*. It is best to know what to do when dealing with strangers. First, always be aware of your surroundings. When you are out and about, take familiar routes. Only take a different path if you are with a trusted adult. It is also a good idea to travel with friends or an adult at all times. If something seems wrong, pay attention. It may be best to leave where you are. For example, you may feel something is wrong if a stranger appears to be following you, whether on foot or in a car. Always trust your instincts. Never take anything from strangers or go for rides with them. Keep in mind that not all strangers look scary or dangerous.

Stick to areas and routes you're familiar with and know to be safe.

Avoid using your cell phone when walking in public so you can be aware of your surroundings.

It is always best to be careful around someone you don't know. Never give

1972

Year the first National Neighborhood Watch program began.

- It is best to stick to familiar environments and to go places with friends.
- Strangers with bad intentions don't always look scary or dangerous.
- Safe strangers include police officers, teachers, principals, and librarians.

personal information to strangers or get close to a strange car. If a stranger asks for directions or help with something, it is best to avoid the situation and head home. If you can't get home, try to find a safe stranger or a safe place. A safe stranger is a trusted adult, such as a police officer, teacher, principal, or librarian. You can ask safe strangers for help when you need it. The same rules can apply to strangers online. Never talk to people you don't know or give away personal information on the Internet. If something feels wrong or dangerous, seek a trusted adult.

Help Prevent Sports Injuries

Participating in any kind of sport or physical activity is fun. It's also a great way to get exercise. However, there is always the risk of injury when playing sports. You should always wear protective gear. Helmets should be worn when playing sports that involve contact and speed. These sports include baseball, football, hockey, biking, and skating. Other sports may require other gear as well. For instance, hockey players must wear face masks so that pucks and hockey sticks cannot hit their faces. Soccer players wear shin guards since so much of the sport consists of kicking. Specialized shoes, mouth guards, and even shatterproof glasses are all good sports gear. Make sure your equipment fits correctly.

You can prevent sports injuries through consistent practice and warming up before playing. A warm-up prepares your muscles and body for exercise and puts

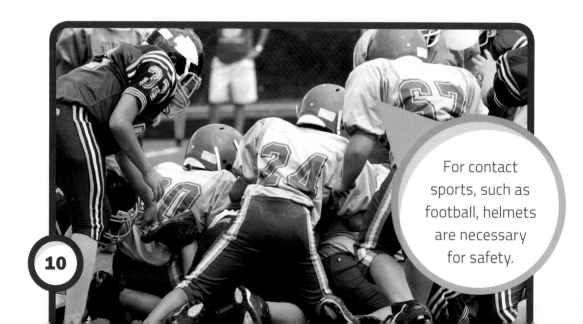

For contact sports, such as football, helmets are necessary for safety.

3.5 million

Estimated number of people under age 14 who need medical treatment for sports injuries each year.

- Protective sports gear should be worn when playing sports.
- When playing sports, it's possible to develop overuse injuries from using the same muscles over and over.
- To avoid injury always warm up before games and get adequate rest afterward.

CONCUSSIONS

Wearing a helmet during sports activities can help prevent concussions. A concussion is a traumatic brain injury that can change the way your brain works. The brain can move around inside the skull. If the brain slams into the skull due to force, a concussion can occur.

Warm up before and cool down after practicing or playing sports to help prevent muscle injuries.

less stress on your heart. Warming up also puts less stress on joints and tendons, so injury is less likely. Resting between practices and games is also important when playing sports. Sometimes a person can develop overuse injuries. These are injuries caused from using the same muscles over and over. If you experience an overuse injury, it may be best to relax until you are fully healed.

Learn about Water Safety

Swimming on a hot day, whether at the beach or a pool, is a fun activity. It is best to take some precautions before joining in the watery fun. If you don't know how to swim, take swimming lessons. Or at least know your limitations. Life vests and floatation devices should always be worn when boating or taking part in water sports or activities. Wearing a life vest is also a good idea if you are not a strong swimmer and the water reaches depths above your head.

Never swim, kayak, or canoe alone. Avoid running around a pool so you don't slip, and never dive into shallow water, no matter where you are swimming. If you are swimming outside and the weather turns dark and rainy, stay out of the water in case lightning strikes.

Swimming in a lake or ocean is different from swimming in a pool. There are dangers such as uneven lake bottoms

It's never too late to take swimming lessons to become a stronger swimmer.

When kayaking or canoeing, do so with at least one other person.

and currents in open water that you might not expect. Don't swim without a lifeguard or parent nearby. Play it safe and wear foot protection, even when swimming. This will protect you from sharp rocks, glass, or other debris that may be in the water. If you are kayaking or canoeing, always be sure you and your fellow rowers know the area or have a map.

HOW TO SWIM OUT OF A RIPTIDE

A riptide is a current. It forms when water built up on shore floats back into open water. This happens most often around piers or docks of oceans or large lakes. Being caught in a riptide can feel like it is pulling you away from shore. If this happens, don't panic. Swim parallel to shore until you clear the current. Swimming against the current will only tire you out. If you can't swim away from the current, let yourself float with it. Soon it will slow down, and you can swim back to shore.

1

Age a child should be before taking swimming lessons, according to the American Association of Pediatrics.

- Take swimming lessons to learn how to swim in deep water.
- Wear a life vest whenever boating or taking part in water sports and activities.
- Wear foot protection when swimming in open water to protect against debris.

Plan an Escape Route in Case of a Fire

Home fires are dangerous and can spread quickly. Being prepared and knowing what to do in case of a fire will help you escape. The first step in fire preparedness is having smoke alarms installed. Be familiar with the sound of a smoke detector. If it beeps, it is time to change out the battery. Never neglect a smoke alarm that needs maintenance. Never ignore a detector if it goes off. Even if you do not see, smell, or hear fire, there may be one starting.

You and your family should create an escape plan. Have an escape route from every room in your home. Figure out at least two ways out of every room. Practice each escape plan with a timer. In case of an actual fire, feel your doorknob and door to see if they are hot. If fire is blazing on the other side, you will have to use your alternate exit. Smoke from a fire is very toxic. It contains poisonous gases and chemicals that can make you drowsy and confused.

Make sure every bedroom and level in your home has a working smoke detector.

THINK ABOUT IT

How do you think people in apartments get out safely if there is a fire? How do students in a university classroom escape a fire? Research the answers to these questions. How do those safety rules compare to your safety plans at school?

2

Number of times per year the battery in a smoke detector should be changed.

- Never ignore the alarm from a smoke detector.
- When planning an escape route, always find at least two ways out of a room.
- If you are escaping from a fire, keep low to the ground to avoid inhaling smoke.

If you are escaping a burning building, stay low to the ground to avoid inhaling smoke. Smoke rises, so it will be less thick close to the ground.

Help prevent a fire from ever happening in your home. Never handle matches or lighters, and remember to blow out any lit candles when you leave the room. Don't plug too many cords into outlets. If space heaters are used in your home, keep them in an open area. Remember to turn off or unplug space heaters when you're not in the room.

PROTECT YOURSELF

If a smoke detector goes off in your home and you see fire and smell smoke, follow these three rules: Get out. Stay out. Call for help. As you leave your home, cover your mouth with a wet cloth or piece of clothing. This will help prevent you from inhaling smoke and fumes. Never stop to take possessions with you, and don't call 911 until you are safely outside. If your clothes catch fire, stop, drop, and roll as soon as possible to put out the flames.

Know What to Do in Weather Emergencies

No matter where you live, it is wise to be familiar with the seasons and weather patterns in your area. Talk with your family about creating an emergency kit for possible weather emergencies. An emergency kit should have enough supplies for your family for at least three days. Another good idea is to have a communication plan. If a weather emergency strikes suddenly, you may not be with your family. Make plans on how to connect with one another and where to meet.

Learning how to stay safe during a weather emergency is key. During a severe thunderstorm, keep a battery-operated radio nearby. If you lose power, the radio will allow you to listen to the latest news and weather updates. Sometimes people are advised to evacuate when a hurricane is expected. If you stay home during a hurricane, be sure to cover the windows. Let family and friends know where you are, and

Create an emergency kit list and gather supplies with your family for possible weather emergencies.

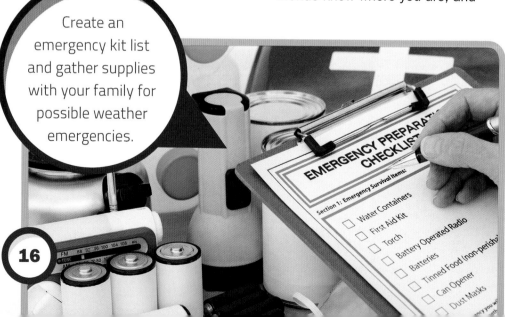

EMERGENCY PREPARAT
CHECKLIST

Section 1: Emergency Survival Items:

☐ Water Containers
☐ First Aid Kit
☐ Torch
☐ Battery Operated Radio
☐ Batteries
☐ Tinned Food (non-perisha
☐ Can Opener
☐ Dust Masks

keep the TV or radio tuned to the news for up-to-date forecasts. If you live where tornadoes often strike, know whether or not you will go to a basement, storm cellar, or safe room in your home. If you know a tsunami is on the way, evacuate immediately. Move away from the coastline and get to higher ground as soon as possible.

If a hurricane is expected in your area, help board up windows to protect your home.

If you are indoors during an earthquake, drop to the floor. Crawl beneath a table or desk. Stay away from windows or heavy furniture that might fall over. If you are outdoors, get away from buildings, trees, and power lines. Find a clear spot to drop down and wait for the quake to end.

3,786
Approximate average number of earthquakes per year in the United States from 2000 to 2012.

- Learn your area's weather patterns.
- Your emergency kit should have enough supplies to last your family for three days.
- Keep a battery-operated radio in an easy-to-locate place for when weather emergencies occur.

THINK ABOUT IT

Imagine you are out walking when a thunderstorm strikes. You see lightning, and you are a mile from home. What is the best thing you can do for your safety? Use another source to help formulate your answer.

Be Prepared for Extreme Heat or Cold

Many of us are able to dress appropriately for hot and cold weather. Many of us also have furnaces to heat our homes and air conditioners to cool them. However, if you find yourself outdoors in extreme weather, you should know how to deal with it.

High temperatures can cause harm to the human body. If the human body becomes too warm, it can suffer heat exhaustion or heatstroke. Most human bodies have a core temperature of 98.6°F (37°C). If your body reaches 104°F (40°C), you may experience heatstroke. The first line of defense against overheating is

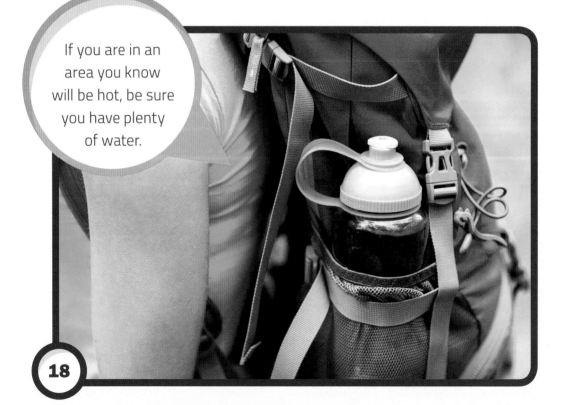

If you are in an area you know will be hot, be sure you have plenty of water.

to drink lots of fluids. Always have a supply of water with you. When sweating in extreme heat, try to replace your electrolytes with a sports drink. Avoid playing or working outdoors during extreme heat.

In very cold weather, and especially with windchill, a person's body can become easily chilled. Exposed flesh can develop frostbite. If a person's body temperature drops too low, an inability to move can occur. The person may also suffer from shallow breathing. To keep warm, wear many layers of warm clothing. A hat will prevent heat loss from the head. A scarf will help keep cold air from getting into the lungs if you use it

0

Temperature, in degrees Fahrenheit (-17.8°C), at which a body becomes susceptible to frostbite, especially with windchill.

- If a person becomes too warm, heat exhaustion or heatstroke can occur.
- On very cold days, a person's exposed flesh can develop frostbite.
- Appropriate clothing such as mittens, scarves, and hats will prevent loss of body heat in cold weather.

to cover your mouth. And be sure to wear heavy socks and mittens.

In extreme cold, it's crucial to protect every inch of skin from the elements.

Safely Enjoy the Outdoors

Hiking and camping are fun and exciting ways to explore the outdoors. Keeping some safety tips in mind while enjoying these activities will make your experience even better.

When hiking, always have a friend or two with you. Bring along a map of the trail you are hiking. Start out slowly on your hike and don't attempt a trail that is too difficult. Your gear should include water, snacks, sunscreen, a cell phone, and a small first-aid kit. Wear hiking boots and pay attention to the terrain. The trail may be bumpy or have obstacles, such as rocks or tree branches, in the way. Most importantly, check the weather before planning a hike.

When choosing a site to camp, be sure you are not in an area that floods. It is a good idea to have at least two hours of daylight to pitch your tent and set up

Keep an eye on the weather before your hike. If conditions are poor, consider hiking another day.

40 million

Approximate number of people who went camping in the United States in 2013.

- Always go hiking with friends or adults.
- Hiking boots are important to wear when hiking on trails.
- Never leave food out in the open when camping.

THINK ABOUT IT

Use books or other sources to find out how many national parks are in the United States. How many allow hiking and camping? Are any of them near you? If not, what other trails and campsites in your area could you explore? Make a list of all of the gear you will need for your trip.

camp. Sometimes you may have to deter insects such as bees, hornets, and wasps. Avoid wearing strong scents, such as perfume or cologne, that might attract the insects. Another thing to keep in mind is the wildlife—big or small. Know the steps you should take if you encounter any. Many animals are attracted to food and garbage. Be sure to dispose of your garbage correctly. Never leave food out in the open. Store it in airtight containers. Finally, learn about dangerous plants around your campsite. Once you are familiar with plants such as poison ivy or poison oak, you can avoid them.

NEED FOR SUNSCREEN

The Skin Cancer Foundation recommends that everyone six months and older wear sunscreen every day. Many people remember to wear sunscreen on hot, sunny days so they don't get sunburned. Sunscreen should also be worn on cloudy days. Up to 40 percent of the sun's ultraviolet rays can still reach Earth on a cloudy day, which means you can still burn.

Understand Indoor and Outdoor Electricity

Electricity is a part of our everyday lives. It helps light and heat our homes. Unfortunately, electricity can cause burns, shocks, and even death. Learning a few safeguards about electricity will help keep you safe. Always handle electrical cords with care. Never remove a plug by pulling on the cord. Avoid using anything with damaged wires or cords and try to keep cords neatly arranged. Tangled cords lying around can cause a fall or another accident. Only use electrical items in the bathroom that belong there, such as hair dryers and electric toothbrushes. Even then, be careful to keep all cords away from water.

When outdoors, know how to avoid dangerous electrical situations.

When unplugging a cord, remove the base of the cord from the outlet instead of pulling on the cord.

Benjamin Franklin was one of the first people to experiment with electricity.

For instance, never fly a kite near electrical power lines. Keep outdoor electrical cords away from water. Stay away from transformers or utility boxes. These usually store underground power lines. Climbing trees can be fun, but don't climb any that are near power lines. If power lines ever fall to the ground, keep your distance from them. Have an adult call for help.

10,932
Amount of kilowatt-hours the average US home used in 2014.

- Handle all electrical cords with care.
- Keep all electrical cords away from water.
- When outside, never climb trees or fly kites near power lines.

BENJAMIN FRANKLIN

Founding father Benjamin Franklin is famous for an experiment he conducted in Philadelphia, Pennsylvania, in 1752. He wanted to prove that lightning was an electric spark. He flew a kite during a thunderstorm and electrically charged the string through a lightning strike. He also invented the lightning rod. Lightning rods are placed on top of buildings to protect them from lightning strikes.

Use Caution with Pets

Many families own pets. Maybe your family has a dog. Or perhaps your friend has a cat. Pets can be a fun addition to a family. Many people find great companionship with cats, dogs, or other animals. Being aware of how animals react to certain situations can go a long way in keeping you and your pet safe.

Never bother a pet when it is eating or sleeping. It may become startled and try to protect itself. When you pet an animal, always do so gently and never pull its tail, ears, or fur.

It is best to leave pets alone while they eat, as some pets are protective over their food.

Follow these same guidelines with your friends' pets.

If you see a strange dog, do not go near it, even if it looks friendly. An excited dog is more likely to jump or scratch, so it's a good idea not to touch it. Know the signs of an aggressive dog: lips snarling back, hair raised. In such a case, do not make direct eye contact. Do not run away. Dogs like to chase moving things. Instead, back away slowly. If you approach a cat, always do so quietly and gently. If a dog or cat bites or scratches you, be sure to wash the wound carefully. Even pet birds can bite. Some birds can carry what is called parrot fever. Always wash your hands after handling a bird.

54.4 million

Number of US households that owned at least one dog in 2014.

- Family pets can be a great source of companionship.
- Never bother an animal that is eating or sleeping.
- Learning what aggressive behavior looks like in dogs can help keep you safe.

Wash your hands after petting animals or handling pet treats or food.

Learn about Food Safety

Food safety is important and can help prevent you and your family from getting a foodborne illness. Some of these illnesses include E. coli, salmonella, and listeria, which can all cause abdominal cramps, vomiting, and dehydration. When at the grocery store, do not buy fruit with broken skin, since bacteria can get in that way. Avoid broken eggs and dented cans. Never buy meat that smells or looks strange, even if the date on the label says it is fresh.

When putting groceries away, follow a few simple rules. Keep cold items together in the refrigerator. Frozen items should always stay in the freezer until you are ready to use them. Store raw meat separately

Always check labels on food packages for dates to see if the item is still fresh.

from other food in the refrigerator. Before eating or preparing raw fruits and vegetables, wash them with water. If you are making a salad, wash the greens first and then remove the outer leaves. If you ever handle raw meat, be sure to wash your hands with soap and warm water afterward. Wipe down any surfaces the meat may have touched with warm, soapy water. If there are leftovers, refrigerate them as soon as possible so bacteria have no chance to grow.

Food allergies are another aspect of food safety. Many people experience sensitivities to some kinds of food, such as peanuts or dairy products. If you are allergic to something, you can take steps at home and at school to avoid exposure to your food allergens, such as sitting at a peanut-free table in the cafeteria.

Even if a food label says food is fresh, do not purchase food that looks old or odd-colored.

1 in 6

Estimated number of Americans who get sick yearly from foodborne illnesses.

- Properly handling food can greatly reduce your chance of catching a foodborne illness.
- Never buy broken eggs, dented cans, or meat that smells or looks strange.
- Keep cold foods cold and frozen foods frozen.

Fact Sheet

- Playgrounds are great places to get fresh air and to burn off some energy. Everybody wants to have fun when enjoying the playground. Knowing some safety tips will make your time there even more fun. When you get to the playground, look around for garbage, broken glass, or other debris. If you see such conditions, you might not want to play there. Don't climb too high on tall playground equipment, such as slides or jungle gyms. Only go as high as you are comfortable. When you are playing on the swings, make sure no one is in your path. This will prevent collisions. Always bring a friend or two when visiting the playground—the more the merrier!

- Travel safety is an important issue. Whether traveling in a car or on a bus, there are some rules to keep in mind. Kids 13 years old and younger need to sit in the back seat of a car. Seatbelts should be worn at all times to keep you in place if there is an accident. When riding in a car, be sure to sit still and don't goof around. This might distract the driver. When riding on a bus, see if there are seatbelts. If there are, be sure to buckle up before the bus starts moving. If there are no seatbelts on the bus, take care to stay in your seat at all times. When waiting for a bus, stand well away from the curb so the driver can see you.

- When you are old enough to stay home alone, you and your parents should come up with some basic safety rules. Ask parents to leave a list of emergency phone numbers in an easy-to-see place, such as on the refrigerator. Do not open the door to anyone when you are home alone. If someone calls and asks for a parent, it's okay to say, "So-and-so is not able to come to the phone right now; may I take a message?" Be sure to know where there are flashlights and a battery-operated radio in case the power goes out. Also know where the first-aid kit is kept so you can quickly and easily take care of any cuts or scrapes.

29

Glossary

allergens
Substances that cause allergic reactions.

current
The movement of water in a river or ocean.

cyberbullying
Bullying that takes place online.

debris
Scattered or broken pieces of something.

electrolytes
Part of the fluids in the body that processes vitamins and minerals.

evacuate
To move away from an area because it has become dangerous.

frostbite
Damage to parts of the body, such as fingers, toes, or ears, due to extreme cold.

hack
To illegally gain access into someone else's computer system or online information.

terrain
Ground or land.

windchill
A temperature that shows how cold the air feels because of wind.

For More Information

Books

Bellisario, Gina. *Be Aware! My Tips for Personal Safety.* Minneapolis, MN: Millbrook Press, 2014.

Purdie, Kate. *Safety.* New York: PowerKids Press, 2010.

Raatma, Lucia. *Staying Safe Around Fire.* Mankato, MN: Capstone Press, 2012.

Visit 12StoryLibrary.com

Scan the code or use your school's login at **12StoryLibrary.com** for recent updates about this topic and a full digital version of this book. Enjoy free access to:

- Digital ebook
- Breaking news updates
- Live content feeds
- Videos, interactive maps, and graphics
- Additional web resources

Note to educators: Visit 12StoryLibrary.com/register to sign up for free premium website access. Enjoy live content plus a full digital version of every 12-Story Library book you own for every student at your school.

Index

About the Author

Jamie Kallio is a youth services librarian in the south suburbs of Chicago. She is the author of several nonfiction books for kids. When she is not writing or reading, she can be found playing with her Chihuahua mix puppy, Elsa.

READ MORE FROM 12-STORY LIBRARY

Every 12-Story Library book is available in many formats. For more information, visit 12StoryLibrary.com.